Colors
A Woman's Guide for Self-Discovery, Balance, and Bliss

By
Nancy Andres

Align

Publishing LLC

Books for Mind, Body, Spirit

Align Publishing LLC
Tucson, AZ 85710
Email: alignpublishing@aol.com

First Printing 2014 Copyright © 2002 by Nancy Andres

Publisher's Note
The publisher and author do not assume and hereby disclaim any liability to any party for any loss or damage caused by errors or omissions in *Colors of Joy: A Woman's Guide for Self-Discovery, Balance, and Bliss.* This book is designed to provide general information about personal growth and improved well-being, not be a replacement for professional counsel, whether for mental health or medical issues. It is sold with the understanding that the publisher and the author are not engaged in rendering therapeutic or medical advice. Please seek a medical opinion if you have any concerns about your health.

Andres, Nancy
[Colors of Joy]
Colors of Joy: A Woman's Guide for Self-Discovery, Balance, and Bliss/Nancy Andres

ISBN # 978-0-615-93273-6
    1. Self-Help 2. Health and Wellness
    3. Color Energy 4. Journal Writing and Reflection
    5. Women's Studies

Dedication Page

Date _Dec 25, 2015_

This Book is for ♥ _My Partner Joan_

This Book is from ♥ _Your Partner Greg_

Dear _Partner,_

We have chosen our path and
blazed our own trail. This
journey together makes me
the happiest I am ever
read. Thank you Partner.

Colors of Joy ♥ Table of Contents

Section 1

Section 2

Affirm my Thoughts and Claim my Power
My personal beliefs color my life choices.

Revise my Thinking and Evolve and Grow
I adapt well to new situations and adjust easily to changes
in my life.

Savor the Moment and Awaken to Joy
I appreciate my sense of touch, taste, smell, vision, and
hearing.

Reach for the Stars and Dare to Dream
My heart knows life is a wondrous adventure.

Love Myself Unconditionally and Thrive
I cherish and respect myself just as I am.

Nurture Friendships and Enrich my Life
My friendships are supportive and communication is
authentic and respectful.

Section 3

Read First—How This Book Can Help You

Colors of Joy: A Woman's Guide for Self-Discovery, Balance, and Bliss provides many ideas to boost vitality, enhance well-being, and spark delight through journal writing, affirmations, reflection, and color-coded activities. It also presents tips that work to release tension, restore equilibrium, and raise self-esteem.

These techniques have helped me tap into my essence, a place I couldn't reach in any other way. After my dad's death and an estrangement from my adult daughter, spilling my heartache out onto the page helped me accept responsibility for my hurt feelings and share them in an appropriate, caring way.

My career as a Health & Lifestyle Writer and Blogger is fast-paced and exciting. Kay Lesh, Ph.D., who contributed the next segment, Using *Colors of Joy*: A Therapist's View, describes the psychological aspects of colors, affirmations, and journaling. She has found satisfaction and meaning in her career in a private counseling practice for 30 years.

However, we are like most women we know. We juggle work responsibilities with family time, personal pursuits and needs, and our civic and social activities. With this in mind, our experience, training, and research suggests that many of the life practices described in *Colors of Joy* will support you as you gain insights about yourself and affirm your innate goodness.

Dear reader, please ask yourself—Do I like and approve of myself? Is concern for my well- being reflected in the way I set priorities for self-care? Do I yearn to feel contented, centered, and confident more often? Am I willing to explore how colors can help me do this? If you answer yes or even maybe, please read to the end of Page 14.

After that page, the book is a twelve week program that can be done in any order and at a pace that works best for you. Try taking a lighthearted approach and think of this guide as the gateway to new adventures.

Skim through the pages of *Colors of Joy* or turn to the Table of Contents to decide where to start. For example, go to Chapter 2 on Page 26. It features green, pink, and yellow. Gaze at the colored insert at the beginning. It was specifically chosen to correspond to the theme (title) for the week. Green hues symbolize nature and fresh starts. Pink signifies gentleness, and yellow represents good cheer. Together, they create a sense of balance as well as foster growth, kindness, adaptability, and enjoyment.

Perhaps you'd rather turn to the "red energy" that appears on Page 56. Shades of red, rose, and pink are offered to provide a sense of unconditional love and cherishing.

All the chapters have colored inserts. However, if you do not *feel, sense, see,* or *think* a color or colors works for you, trust your intuition. Please imagine ones that resonate in you.

When you write in *Colors of Joy*, start by identifying your mood. Are you happy, sad, angry, lonely, hungry, tense, fearful, excited, enthusiastic, or feel a combination of emotions? Jot down one or more in the mood check-in area. If you prefer, draw a picture to describe your mood. After you complete a page, evaluate your frame of mind. Then, record any shifts in attitude or feelings.

Some women read and reflect on one page a day. Others prefer a less structured approach. Perhaps this book will become a refreshing addition to your early morning routine. Maybe you'd rather devote a few minutes before bedtime to use this book. Sip a cup of herbal tea or cocoa, play soothing music, and journal to release the cares of the day. This guide may be what you need to set the tone for blissful sleep.

Colors of Joy outlines relaxation practices like an easy to learn, one-minute meditation. Meditation can calm overactive thinking and is a helpful way to start each session. Being mindful helps you use the colors, affirmations, and journaling to full advantage. In fact, being in the moment may help you recognize the direct pathway from your breath to your pen, spirit, and body.

Colors of Joy is authored by a woman, with a woman's sensibilities in mind. It describes life skills that can help you understand yourself better as well as improve interactions with others.

This interactive guide introduces at least one affirmation per chapter. It is the statement that follows the chapter title. Each is written in **this playful font**. An affirmation is a declaration that confirms something is already true and bountiful in your life. Repeat affirmations aloud to reinforce their power. Additional affirmations are included in several chapters. Those are *italicized*.

I frequently find that whatever I value and dwell on will materialize or be strengthened (law of attraction and positive reinforcement). Those things I let go of lessen. See whether this is true for you.

If possible, use colored pencils or pens to respond to questions and topics. Observe which colors speak to you.

Consider your surroundings and the colors that attract or repel you. What is the predominant color in your home and your wardrobe? Are you drawn to eat a delectable plum or a juicy piece of orange cantaloupe? Your body instinctively moves toward color harmony and integrates the color vibrations it needs. Studies indicate that colors can help enliven your mood, increase your power of concentration, and soothe or energize you.

Color and light therapy (lasers) are in the forefront of modern surgery and healing. Studies show that the lack of sunlight causes a condition called Seasonal Affective Disorder (SAD). Still other research has documented that colored images help us process and store scenes in the natural world more effectively than black and white ones.

Please continue reading and discover how color helpers/guides, color meditations and visualizations, and the self-help methods detailed in *Colors of Joy* can increase your sense of well-being and good will.

Here are Important Color Guides for You

Green facilitates grounding, growth, and self-acceptance. Walk in a green field or cultivate your garden. Green is a symbol of regeneration and vitality.

Blue soothes and calms. Inhale and exhale deeply and imagine the azure sea or broad expanse of sky. Blue energy helps you unwind and relax. Wear pale blue apparel or use it as an accent color in your office. It creates a sense of peace and stability. Wear royal or navy blue clothing. Use it in your logo, or select deep blue furniture or clothing to present a dignified air.

Orange reduces sadness and combats depression. Wear this color to mend a broken heart. Don an orange tee, when you need to balance hormones.

Violet and **Purple** are symbols of creativity and indicate a dramatic flair. Purple is a royal ray, the ruler, the spiritual master. Wear an amethyst ring or bracelet to feel protected and serene. Place purple flowers beside you at the computer or at your reading area to relieve eye strain.

Red is the primary color associated with passion. It holds our attention and speeds up the body's metabolism. Red is popular among young people in the United States and is often chosen when drawing hearts and flames. Use it for a boost of energy. **Pink** (mixture of red and white) sparks compassion, nurturing, and love.

White is the color that is inclusive of the entire visible light spectrum. It is interpreted differently in various cultures. Some consider white to be the color of beginnings. It can signify purity, as in white for the bride. Others think of white for endings, like the starkness of winter snow and death. Many consider white to connote wholeness, completion, and illumination.

Yellow broadcasts a sunny disposition and wearing it may help you feel alert and flexible. Yellow is a symbol of lightheartedness. When you sense its ability to lift your spirit, you may buy a bunch of yellow flowers like daffodils.

Many activities in *Colors of Joy* urge you to be kind to yourself. Several exercises help you unwind, kick back, and relax. Still others illustrate how to expel trapped energy through physical and mental activity or to reach out to others for encouragement. Perhaps all relate to the following thought: s*elf-care is a <u>privilege</u> only you can grant yourself.*

Colors of Joy gives you a chance to sort through your own self-talk. It urges you to treat yourself respectfully, and describes methods that help you dismiss your inner critic. Learn which attitudes and behaviors allow you to enjoy your work and play, and what inspires you to find your bliss.

What colors attract you? I invite you to use them on a one-day-at-a-time adventure.

♥ Create a Colorful Life♥

♥Free the Joy Within♥

Many Blessings,

Nancy Andres

Using *Colors of Joy* — A Therapist's View

My work as a therapist has confirmed and strengthened my belief that human beings have an innate desire to move toward personal growth and emotional well-being. In the 30 years I have been privileged to work with my clients as a professional counselor, I have seen people make amazing changes, leading them to happier and more productive lives.

When I find a guide I believe people can use to understand themselves better and one that encourages self-actualization, I am delighted. *Colors of Joy* is just such a guide.

Three facets of this book— color, affirmations, and journaling, are grounded in psychological literature. They interact and complement each other to make the time spent with this book both productive and pleasant.

Color is known to affect us psychologically. For example, think of how you feel when you wear a color that is flattering to you. Your mood is elevated and you're likely to get positive comments from others. When you wear a color that isn't flattering, you probably feel washed out and unenergetic, and the lack of response from those around you adds to this feeling. Color affects our mood and our outlook. It also affects the responses we receive from others. Both help to raise or lower our spirits.

Are you aware that busy restaurants use bright, peppy colors like red for the walls and furniture? The owners want you to feel energized, and eat and leave. Fast turnover is their goal. Slower paced restaurants may use muted, relaxing colors of blue and green to invite you to linger and relax. It is helpful to know that color affects us, whether we are consciously aware of it or not.

Frequently one of the first visible signs of change in a client occurs when I see a shift in the colors the person wears. A person who began the therapy process wearing quiet colors—subdued grays, blacks, and navy blues may switch to pastels, as she begins to be more ready to open up to the world. For me, this indicates that the internal work is beginning to show externally. And sometimes, I may recommend the "act as if" phenomenon for a client. That is, I may ask the person to wear brighter colors, even though she may not yet be at a place where it occurs to her to do so. I have seen how attitude follows behavior, and how a simple gesture makes one feel good about oneself and puts a positive spin on the day.

Specific colors are integrated into this book. Colors can heal and rejuvenate energy and they're paired with affirmations to maximize the benefit for you.

Studies show that affirmations allow us to focus our thoughts in a positive way and to gain insights. Writing our affirmations makes them even more powerful. That mind-body-spirit connection is an effective self-empowerment tool and thought (affirmations) followed by action (writing) can lead to positive change.

Religious figures have used journals as a way to record their struggles, doubts, progress, and insights. We know about the lives of pioneer women through their journals. Anne Frank shared her adolescent hopes and fears in her journal as she lived her life in hiding during the Nazi persecution of the Jews in World War II.

Journaling also has been studied in psychology. A recent study compared college students who wrote about an issue of concern to them with a group of students who had a similar concern but did not write. Not surprisingly, the students who wrote about their experiences processed their emotions around these issues more quickly and reported less distress than those who did not. Findings also indicate that journal writing helps access intuitive knowledge and understandings.

As a therapist, I frequently recommend that my clients keep a journal. I've found that journals can be a marvelous adjunct to therapy or a useful stand alone device. As you grow, you can use a journal to record your progress and have a private place to write about your uncertainties as well as your desires and aspirations for the person you are becoming. A journal is also a wonderful way to record and savor successes and pleasures. Spending time each day in quiet meditation and peaceful union with your inner wisdom helps you regain balance and direction in your life. It often results in renewed energy and joy.

This book can be empowering and freeing. Colors boost your experience; affirmations give focus; and journaling allows you to survey your thoughts, feelings, and ideas in a safe environment.

Colors of Joy is planned to help you find ways to rise above some of the old messages and habits that may have been holding you back. Its gentle, caring tone encourages increased self-awareness, compassion, and appreciation. I wish you an exciting journey as you use *Colors of Joy* to move to greater self-knowledge and improved well-being.

Warm regards,

Kay Lesh, Ph.D.

CHAPTER 1

Affirm my Thoughts and Claim my Power

Affirm my Thoughts and Claim my Power
My personal beliefs color my life choices.

♥ ♥

MONDAY

Date_____   Mood Check_____

Take a moment to write down today's date and enter a one or two word description of your mood. Next, think of your favorite color or hue. Envision that color traveling into your body. What parts of your body welcome this color? Can you think of this color as being liquid pleasure? Does this process create a sense of harmony and cheerfulness within you or does it reveal something else? Explain by writing down your feelings, thoughts, and beliefs about your favorite color. Use the space provided below. If you need extra space for journaling, use the reflections page that's provided at the end of this and every chapter. After doing this exercise, re-check your mood. Has it changed or stayed the same? Then, daydream about your favorite color and smile.

Affirm my Thoughts and Claim my Power

My personal beliefs color my life choices.

♥ ♥

TUESDAY

Date_____   Mood Check_____

Please fill in the date and record your mood before you begin. Think about how often you take time for a pleasurable activity during the week. Override any internal taskmaster voices and affirm: *I take excellent care of myself by engaging in a refreshing activity every day.* This week, listen to the music of your favorite vocalist or group, read for entertainment, see a movie or play, visit a friend, or participate in a sport. If you can't come up with any ideas, think about some things your friends enjoy and experiment by doing something you haven't tried before. Write about having fun.

Affirm my Thoughts and Claim my Power
My personal beliefs color my life choices.

♥ ♥

WEDNESDAY

Date_____   Mood Check_____

Today, envision an area in your life that challenges you. In the space below, spell out this challenge in three or four words. Then, draw a line down the middle of the empty space below it. Write PROS on the left and CONS on the right. List all those things that seem productive about this issue, relationship, or situation on the Pro side. List those things that seem draining on the Con side. For today, can you let this situation exist without trying to fix it? Review this section tomorrow and record your observations. If you need more writing space, go to the reflections for the week page that appears at the end of this chapter.

Affirm my Thoughts and Claim my Power
My personal beliefs color my life choices.

♥ ♥

THURSDAY

Date_____   Mood Check_____

Today, list a few ideas to help make your daily routines enjoyable. Think of ways to exercise, clean, organize a closet, shop, or make work-related projects satisfying. Think about a venture you long to start. Take one tiny step toward your goal. Go about the undertaking with an optimistic attitude to cheer yourself along. Remember to congratulate yourself for moving forward, even if you can't complete the task. Then, write about your discoveries. What color symbolizes empowerment to you? Use it now.

Affirm my Thoughts and Claim my Power
My personal beliefs color my life choices.

♥ ♥

FRIDAY

Date_____   Mood Check_____

Do you ever feel pressured to say yes when you mean to say no? Describe a few instances when you made the decision to go against your true nature. Did you feel disappointed or angry with yourself as a result? What would help you pause to evaluate your options, before committing to something you may not really want to do? Explain.

Affirm my Thoughts and Claim my Power
My personal beliefs color my life choices.

♥ ♥

SATURDAY

Date_____   Mood Check_____

Please fill in the date and mood check-in blanks. Then, think about colors that remind you of anger, hurt, guilt, sadness, fear, or apprehension. Use colored pencils, pens, or crayons to illustrate one of those feelings right now. Have you ever "walked it out" or used other forms of exercise to lessen frustration or stress? Try one of the following activities to see whether it releases tension in you. Pound your bed pillow for a few seconds (without hurting your hand) or twist a bath towel to expel trapped energy from your body. What methods have worked well to help you reduce anger or hurt from your mind and body? Jot down four other ways you know that help you discharge stress.

Affirm my Thoughts and Claim my Power

My personal beliefs color my life choices.

♥ ♥

SUNDAY

Date_____   Mood Check_____

Notice what happens when you take a moment to say the next affirmation. *Unfamiliar territory is loaded with possibilities.* Think of the color white. It is made up of all the colors in the visible spectrum and stimulates illumination. Then, create your own self-empowering affirmation by working on it in the space below. Without censoring yourself, write down an affirmation that describes your wisdom, kindness, or willingness to grow. For additional space, use the reflection page that follows.

Affirm my Thoughts and Claim my Power

My personal beliefs color my life choices.

♥♥♥♥♥♥♥♥♥♥♥♥♥♥♥♥♥♥♥♥♥♥♥♥♥

Reflections for the Week

CHAPTER 2
Revise my Thinking and Evolve and Grow

Revise my Thinking and Evolve and Grow

I adapt well to new situations and adjust easily to changes in my life.

♥♥♥♥♥♥♥♥♥♥♥♥♥♥♥♥♥♥♥♥♥♥♥♥♥♥♥

MONDAY

Date_____   Mood Check_____

Write down today's date and record your current mood. Do you think you are flexible and shift gears easily? Gaze at the colors in the picture opposite. Pink, yellow, and green complement each other. When they appear together, they create a sense of harmony. As you write today, describe some methods that have helped you cope with new circumstances or experiences. Keep in mind that green is the color of nature and growth, pink stimulates compassion, and yellow helps you feel lighthearted. Then, journal about any progress you've made in adapting to new things in your life.

Revise my Thinking and Evolve and Grow

I adapt well to new situations and adjust easily to changes in my life.

♥ ♥

TUESDAY

Date_____   Mood Check_____

Jot down today's date and identify your mood. Then, say the affirmation above aloud. This may differ from how you feel right now, especially if you're currently in pain from agitation, physical aches, anger, grief, loss, or fear. Try to imagine a color that helps soothe and comfort you. If you can, explain why this color resonates with you in the space provided. If you'd prefer, draw a picture with calming, reassuring images and colors that help relax you.

Revise my Thinking and Evolve and Grow

I adapt well to new situations and adjust easily to changes in my life.

♥ ♥

WEDNESDAY

Date_____   Mood Check_____

Reflect on the power of your intuition. How has it helped you move forward? If you need more space, use the reflection page at the end of this chapter.

Revise my Thinking and Evolve and Grow

I adapt well to new situations and adjust easily to changes in my life.

♥ ♥

THURSDAY

Date_____   Mood Check_____

When you feel unsure about making a decision, try journaling to help you access your thoughts and feelings. Write about a facet of your life where you think change would be advantageous. Next, state whether you are ready to move forward or have reasons for hesitating. What positive message can you give yourself to remind you that when you're ready, you'll have the courage to act? Write that down too.

Revise my Thinking and Evolve and Grow
I adapt well to new situations and adjust easily to changes in my life.

♥ ♥

FRIDAY

Date_____   Mood Check_____

Every experience is an opportunity for learning. Set the intention to be gentle, patient, and supportive of yourself during transitional times. Think of the color pink as you do this. It stimulates loving kindness. Then, imagine how you would feel if you were able to detach from a situation or relationship that stresses you. Write about one technique you've learned that helps you let go of other people, places, and things. One of my favorites is to affirm, "Mind your own business and the rest will take care of itself."

Revise my Thinking and Evolve and Grow

I adapt well to new situations and adjust easily to changes in my life.

♥ ♥

SATURDAY

Date_____   Mood Check_____

Set the priority to exercise, eat right, sleep in, and read an inspiring book to renew a lagging spirit. This works well, especially to relieve stress. If need be, retire worn out messages that say you must be "continually in motion" and "on the job." Choose balance instead. Perhaps you can reserve ten minutes today (mark it on your calendar) to tap dance or fly a kite, just because it's fun and entertaining. Make a list of several things that relax or amuse you. Do at least five of them in the coming week.

Revise my Thinking and Evolve and Grow

I adapt well to new situations and adjust easily to changes in my life.

♥ ♥

SUNDAY

Date_____   Mood Check_____

Trust and patience in your process will help you wait for the results of your hard work to become visible. Recite this affirmation aloud: *all is well in my life.* Then, reflect on a mantra (a mantra is a word or phrase that is repeated silently or aloud). Use it to tap into the strength in your powerful mind. One mantra that helps center me is "peace, peace, peace." Draw or write about whatever enters your mind now.

Revise my Thinking and Evolve and Grow

I adapt well to new situations and adjust easily to changes in my life.

♥♥♥♥♥♥♥♥♥♥♥♥♥♥♥♥♥♥♥♥♥♥♥♥♥♥

Reflections for the Week

CHAPTER 3
Savor the Moment and Awaken to Joy

Savor the Moment and Awaken to Joy

I appreciate my sense of touch, taste, smell, vision, and hearing.

♥♥♥♥♥♥♥♥♥♥♥♥♥♥♥♥♥♥♥♥♥♥♥♥♥

MONDAY

Date_____   Mood Check_____

Please jot down the date and identify your mood. Don't forget to record it in the space provided. If you frequently worry about the future or dwell on the past, you miss "Now." Try using a meditation technique to anchor yourself into the present moment. Focus on a candle light, imagine your favorite flower, envision a soothing color like sky blue, or listen to the sound of your breath. Sit comfortably, close your eyes, or lie down. Attempt to accept whatever is in your mind and then let the thought go. Practice meditating each day this week. If this is new to you, start with one minute of quiet time and gradually build up to three. Use the space below to describe your meditation concerns.

Savor the Moment and Awaken to Joy

I appreciate my sense of touch, taste, smell, vision, and hearing.

♥ ♥

TUESDAY

Date_____   Mood Check_____

When you feel overwhelmed with projects, pause to inhale and exhale deeply. Today write a "to-do" list with only one thing on your list. Embark on this one task only. When you're finished with it, do another. If you find you are unable to make progress or complete a task in less than an hour, move on to another. Go back later, and reevaluate whether you want to continue on the same path, need to drop it, or can look at the task from a different perspective. When you force an issue, you create stress. Does this information help you? Explain.

Savor the Moment and Awaken to Joy

I appreciate my sense of touch, taste, smell, vision, and hearing.

♥♥♥♥♥♥♥♥♥♥♥♥♥♥♥♥♥♥♥♥♥♥♥♥♥♥

WEDNESDAY

Date_____   Mood Check_____

Today, take a walk in nature. It doesn't matter if it's raining or you have only five minutes of free time. Keep your head where your feet are. Let your body define the word "grounded."

Savor the Moment and Awaken to Joy

I appreciate my sense of touch, taste, smell, vision, and hearing.

♥ ♥

THURSDAY

Date_____   Mood Check_____

Eat a few grapes or raisins, one at a time. Savor the flavor, texture, smell, sound, and sight of eating. Use your senses to take in every detail of this process that you can. Notice what happens to your mind and mood as you do this. Write about your thoughts and emotions or sketch a picture about it, if you care to.

Savor the Moment and Awaken to Joy

I appreciate my sense of touch, taste, smell, vision, and hearing.

♥ ♥

FRIDAY

Date_____   Mood Check_____

If your mind races, practice being a compassionate observer in your own life. Notice how you behave when you have unstructured time. See what comes up for you when you say, *I am in tune with the universe and feel vitally alive in this moment.* Journal about why you think snoozing is a healthy pastime. Choose a color to represent your mood and detail that too.

Savor the Moment and Awaken to Joy

I appreciate my sense of touch, taste, smell, vision, and hearing.

♥ ♥

SATURDAY

Date_____   Mood Check_____

Make a list of <u>all</u> the things you did yesterday. Check those things you rushed through. Star those things you enjoyed. Put a circle around those items you procrastinated over or worried about. Would you be willing to get up earlier or go to bed later to redo one of the checked items? Do you think you have unrealistic expectations of yourself? Whose expectations are they? Explain.

Savor the Moment and Awaken to Joy

I appreciate my sense of touch, taste, smell, vision, and hearing.

♥ ♥

SUNDAY

Date_____   Mood Check_____

Write this phrase; "I'm grateful for… " and finish the sentence. See how it feels. Then, answer this question—*how can an attitude of gratitude benefit me?*

Savor the Moment and Awaken to Joy

I appreciate my sense of touch, taste, smell, vision, and hearing.

♥♥♥♥♥♥♥♥♥♥♥♥♥♥♥♥♥♥♥♥♥♥♥♥♥

Reflections for the Week

CHAPTER 4

Reach for the Stars and Dare to Dream

Reach for the Stars and Dare to Dream

My heart knows life is a wondrous adventure.

♥ ♥

MONDAY

Date_____   Mood Check_____

Do you have aspirations for your career, standard of living, health, relationships, community, and planet? List two areas in your life that you want to improve. Envision Amethyst, a lovely purple-colored form of quartz. This jewel tone stimulates visions and dreams. Then without self-judgment or restraint, write about what your ideal life would look like. If you need more space, go to the reflections page at the end of this chapter.

Reach for the Stars and Dare to Dream
My heart knows life is a wondrous adventure.

♥ ♥

TUESDAY

Date_____   Mood Check_____

Imagine (picture) a few ways you can further the longings of your heart. Try to be spontaneous. Consider ideas you haven't been open to before. You can gain inspiration by asking a friend for suggestions or brainstorming with people or groups that are skilled in a particular arena. For example, you may find it helpful to consult with a financial advisor, lawyer, doctor, marriage counselor, career advisor, or other expert. Write down five things that may motivate you to move forward. Then, give yourself permission to do one today.

Reach for the Stars and Dare to Dream

My heart knows life is a wondrous adventure.

♥ ♥

WEDNESDAY

Date_____   Mood Check_____

Record the date and your mood please. What emotions surface when you think of risk? Are you happy, excited, resistant, or afraid? Identifying and acknowledging your feelings deepens self-knowledge and transformation. Use the journal space below to describe how you feel about risk-taking. After you journal, evaluate your mood. Has it changed? Please record that too.

Reach for the Stars and Dare to Dream
My heart knows life is a wondrous adventure.

♥ ♥

THURSDAY

Date_____   Mood Check_____

Do you realize to further your goals, even baby steps add up? Take at least one small action today in the right direction. Read a book about your dream goal or interview someone who already does this thing. Here's a fun project to do that has helped me. Assemble a collage made out of magazine bits and pieces that show women taking empowering actions. Search for magazine words to include like happy, process, progress, journey, goals, and adventure. Paste them into your collage too. Look at it daily. Write about what personal growth means to you today.

Reach for the Stars and Dare to Dream
My heart knows life is a wondrous adventure.

♥ ♥

FRIDAY

Date_____   Mood Check_____

Do you procrastinate, worry about making mistakes, and find fault with activities you undertake? Each choice you make can lay the foundation for success, as long as you learn from it. What risks are you willing to take today? Write about it.

Reach for the Stars and Dare to Dream

My heart knows life is a wondrous adventure.

♥ ♥

SATURDAY

Date_____   Mood Check_____

After you attend to your daily responsibilities, do you still have energy and time to pursue your bliss? Make a list of activities you love, especially those you haven't done in a long time. Do one of these activities each day, during the next five days. If this seems too much of a challenge, explain.

Reach for the Stars and Dare to Dream

My heart knows life is a wondrous adventure.

♥ ♥

SUNDAY

Date_____   Mood Check_____

You are a precious individual. What traits do you possess that you consider assets? List them. Know you serve a Higher Purpose by allowing your unique self to shine. Does this resonate with you? Explain.

Reach for the Stars and Dare to Dream

My heart knows life is a wondrous adventure.

♥♥♥♥♥♥♥♥♥♥♥♥♥♥♥♥♥♥♥♥♥♥♥♥♥

Reflections for the Week

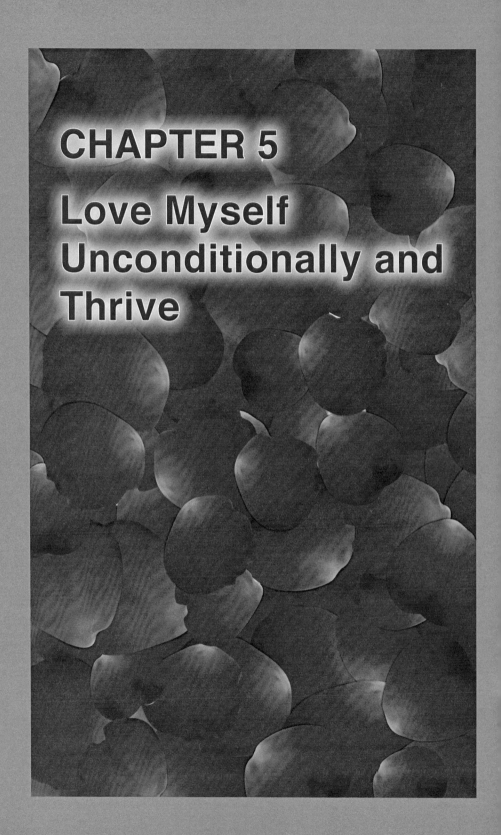

CHAPTER 5
Love Myself Unconditionally and Thrive

Love Myself
Unconditionally and Thrive
I cherish and respect myself just as I am.

♥ ♥

MONDAY

Date_____   Mood Check_____

Contemplate complete self-acceptance. While your eyes are closed, visualize the color pink. If this feels uncomfortable for you, gaze out softly. Give yourself permission to embrace everything about who you believe yourself to be. What positive statement (affirmation) can you write down that illustrates your strengths as a human being? Include traits like gentleness, passion, spontaneity, maturity, love, and caring. Say your affirmation aloud, at least five times today and tomorrow.

Love Myself Unconditionally and Thrive
I cherish and respect myself just as I am.

♥ ♥

TUESDAY

Date_____   Mood Check_____

Today, take a moment to list unique qualities about yourself. Do you have a sense of humor, gift of gab, or skill at cooking or storytelling? Today, reflect about or meditate on one of your admirable traits. What ideas or feelings come up when you do this exercise? Write about it please.

Love Myself
Unconditionally and Thrive
I cherish and respect myself just as I am.

♥ ♥

WEDNESDAY

Date_____   Mood Check_____

When you make a decision (commitment) to yourself to achieve something and follow through to completion, do you delight in your success? Think of two times you were able to reach a goal. Write about what you learned along the way.

Love Myself Unconditionally and Thrive
I cherish and respect myself just as I am.

♥ ♥

THURSDAY

Date_____   Mood Check_____

Do you practice gratitude often? Can you focus on it today?
Write about your blessings. Don't forget to check your mood
before and after doing this.

Love Myself Unconditionally and Thrive
I cherish and respect myself just as I am.

♥ ♥

FRIDAY

Date_____   Mood Check_____

Do you use your talents and skills in your everyday life or do you play down your assets? What would it take for you to let others see the real you more often?

Love Myself Unconditionally and Thrive

I cherish and respect myself just as I am.

♥ ♥

SATURDAY

Date_____   Mood Check_____

Do you feel worthy of respect and caring from others? Explain. Are you respectful and caring with yourself? Do you believe that the way you treat yourself influences your mood, choices, and how others treat you? Describe your thoughts and feelings about this now. If you prefer, look at the colored insert that starts this chapter. Then, come back to this page when you're ready to write about unconditional love.

Love Myself
Unconditionally and Thrive
I cherish and respect myself just as I am.

♥ ♥

SUNDAY

Date_____   Mood Check_____

I am <u>*extraordinary*</u> *exactly the way I am.* Do you "feel" this affirmation in your total being? Today, choose a colored pencil or crayon in a color that pleases you to write about this concept. If you have doubts, say the affirmation above, while feeling compassion for yourself. Please repeat: ***I am Loveable*** several times. Then, write down your thoughts and feelings about self-love.

Love Myself
Unconditionally and Thrive

I cherish and respect myself
just as I am.

♥ ♥

Reflections for the Week

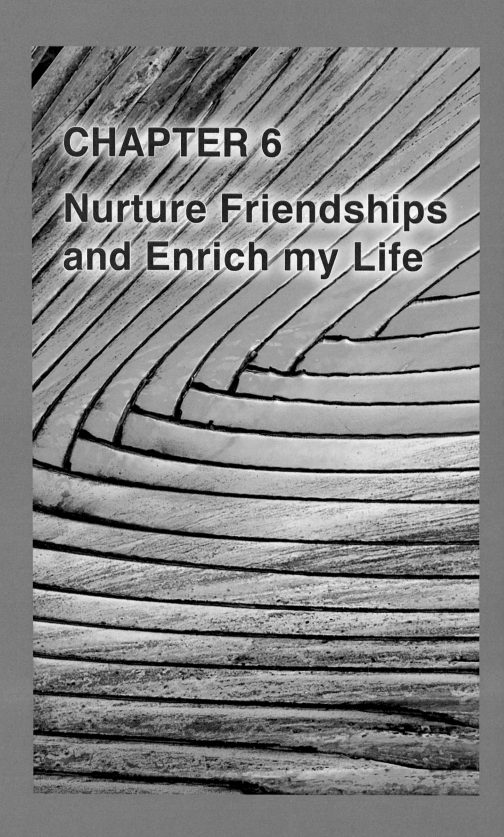

CHAPTER 6
Nurture Friendships and Enrich my Life

Nurture Friendships and Enrich my Life

My friendships are supportive and communication is authentic and respectful.

♥ ♥

MONDAY

Date_____   Mood Check_____

Do you make new friends as well as maintain fulfilling relationships with longtime pals? Think of the important friendships in your life. What color or colors would you use to describe each? Explain.

Nurture Friendships and Enrich my Life

My friendships are supportive and communication is authentic and respectful.

♥ ♥

TUESDAY

Date_____   Mood Check_____

When you feel misunderstood, slighted, angry, or unheard by a friend, do you cope by resorting to blame, judgment, or denial? Do you realize you play a role in every situation? Can you love yourself completely, even when you are unable to get the other person to honor your needs? Explain how it makes you feel, when you realize you need to take responsibility for your part in a conflict with someone else. If you run out of space, go to the reflections section at the end of the chapter.

Nurture Friendships and Enrich my Life

My friendships are supportive and communication is authentic and respectful.

♥ ♥

WEDNESDAY

Date_____   Mood Check_____

What qualities do you possess that contribute to your friendships? When your friends need you to be there for them, are you available to them? What traits do your friends have that you value? Explain.

Nurture Friendships and Enrich my Life

My friendships are supportive and communication is authentic and respectful.

♥ ♥

THURSDAY

Date_____   Mood Check_____

Do you expect friends to support, encourage, and help you in specific ways? When you ask for help from others, be direct. However, you set yourself up for disappointment if you have expectations. As often as you can, tap into your store of self-compassion and shower yourself with attention. Notice how you feel when you are there for yourself. Write about these ideas now.

Nurture Friendships and Enrich my Life

My friendships are supportive and communication is authentic and respectful.

♥ ♥

FRIDAY

Date_____   Mood Check_____

Have you ever noticed that what troubles you most about someone else may be where you feel most vulnerable or unfulfilled? Why do you think this happens? What can you learn from this? Write about each now.

Nurture Friendships and Enrich my Life

My friendships are supportive and communication is authentic and respectful.

♥ ♥

SATURDAY

Date_____   Mood Check_____

Effective communication is powerful. When you need to set a boundary with someone, be direct, concise, and kind. Speak from the "I" as in I need, I want, I prefer you to. Then, give the other person time to process what you've said. If she or he doesn't reply after several moments, can you politely ask whether they need more clarification or time to think? Expand on the topic of setting limits by writing about it today.

Nurture Friendships and Enrich my Life

My friendships are supportive and communication is authentic and respectful.

♥ ♥

SUNDAY

Date_____   Mood Check_____

Focus on this affirmation–*I love unconditionally and my heart overflows with joy.* Write about what this affirmation means to you or compose your own. Think of white (the color of pure energy) and describe ways you will strive to be kinder and more loving with yourself and others.

Nurture Friendships and Enrich my Life

My friendships are supportive and communication is authentic and respectful.

♥♥♥♥♥♥♥♥♥♥♥♥♥♥♥♥♥♥♥♥♥♥♥♥

Reflections for the Week

CHAPTER 7

Release the Past and Tame Old Fears

Release the Past and Tame Old Fears

I accept my family and heal my past.

♥ ♥

MONDAY

Date_____   Mood Check_____

Accepting what is real does not necessarily mean liking it. Today, cultivate an attitude of gratitude. Give thanks to your parents for the gift of life. What traits or skills do you possess that spring from experiences interacting with your family of origin? Write about this topic now.

Release the Past and Tame Old Fears

I accept my family and heal my past.

♥ ♥

TUESDAY

Date_____   Mood Check_____

Envision the color orange and imagine yourself absorbing its health promoting, restorative energies. Conceive of yourself wrapped in a soft blanket of orange as you release or say good-bye to emotional, physical, spiritual, or mental wounds you experienced during your lifetime. Breathe in and out deeply. Think of liberation, relief, and freedom. What do these words and the color orange mean to you? Write about them now please.

Release the Past and Tame Old Fears

I accept my family and heal my past.

♥ ♥

WEDNESDAY

Date_____   Mood Check_____

Did childhood happenings contribute to making you strong, resourceful, loving, kind, generous, wise, persistent, or other character traits you consider assets? Pretend traits are colors. What colors do you imagine these traits to be? Jot down instances when you've transcended the past. In addition, be sure to state why you feel proud about yourself.

Release the Past and Tame Old Fears

I accept my family and heal my past.

♥ ♥

THURSDAY

Date_____   Mood Check_____

Do you allow your children to make age appropriate choices and decisions? Do you agree that it's important for them to take responsibility for their own actions? Explain. If this does not apply to you, do you care for the "inner" youngster inside yourself? Who is she? Explain.

Release the Past and Tame Old Fears
I accept my family and heal my past.

♥ ♥

FRIDAY

Date_____   Mood Check_____

Do you frequently tell your children, spouse, siblings, and parents that you love them? Do your actions toward each match your words? Do family members treat you well? Describe how you express (verbalize) and show (action) love. If you prefer, write about the topic of your choice today.

Release the Past and Tame Old Fears

I accept my family and heal my past.

♥ ♥

SATURDAY

Date_____   Mood Check_____

Is it important to you that your family unit be strong and unified? What can you contribute to making time spent with family more meaningful for you? What specific things would you like to alter in yourself that would help you appreciate your family even more than you do now? Jot those ideas down now.

Release the Past and Tame Old Fears

I accept my family and heal my past.

♥ ♥

SUNDAY

Date_____   Mood Check_____

Envision your family life exactly as it exists today. Write about ways you can improve your attitude toward family members. You can't change others, but you can change your reaction to their behavior or attitudes. Write about this now.

Release the Past and Tame Old Fears

I accept my family and heal my past.

♥♥♥♥♥♥♥♥♥♥♥♥♥♥♥♥♥♥♥♥♥♥♥♥♥

Reflections for the Week

CHAPTER 8
Share my Blessings and Serve a Greater Good

Share my Blessings and Serve a Greater Good

I offer my skills, talents, and time freely and joy flows through me.

♥ ♥

MONDAY

Date_____   Mood Check_____

Think of shell pink and baby blue. Imagine yourself wearing a cloak made of those colors. Then, recall a time when you were able to give freely and wholeheartedly. Note what occurs, when you wear an imaginary coat of bright colors instead of soft ones to envision the same time. Please journal about this experiment or draw a sketch that shows your heart is opening.

Share my Blessings and Serve a Greater Good
I offer my skills, talents, and time freely and joy flows through me.

♥ ♥

TUESDAY

Date_____   Mood Check_____

What motivates you to help others? Is it easier for you to be generous with strangers in need than to those closest to you or the reverse? Examine your thoughts and feelings about both sides of this issue. Remember to do the mood check before and after this activity.

Share my Blessings and Serve a Greater Good

I offer my skills, talents, and time freely and joy flows through me.

♥ ♥

WEDNESDAY

Date_____   Mood Check_____

Envision the color violet. It can help you gain self-knowledge and spiritual awareness. Then, think about whether you often put your need to care for others before your responsibility to meet your own needs. Have you noticed that when you care for yourself first, you are more fully available to help others? Describe how you feel about this.

Share my Blessings and Serve a Greater Good
I offer my skills, talents, and time freely and joy flows through me.

♥ ♥

THURSDAY

Date_____   Mood Check_____

Service to others may be as simple as a smile or a conscious decision not to say a hurtful word. Do you think you are nonjudgmental? Note your first reaction to this question. Then, write about your ability to love today.

Share my Blessings and Serve a Greater Good

I offer my skills, talents, and time freely and joy flows through me.

♥ ♥

FRIDAY

Date_____   Mood Check_____

Have you listened carefully to someone within the last day or two? Do you acknowledge and thank friends, family, colleagues, or acquaintances when they listen closely to you? The gratitude factor contributes to a joyous circle of sharing. Are you comfortable receiving attention as well as giving it? Explain.

Share my Blessings and Serve a Greater Good

I offer my skills, talents, and time freely and joy flows through me.

♥ ♥

SATURDAY

Date_____   Mood Check_____

Everything on our planet is interrelated. What we give out comes back to us in some form or way. Do you make a difference in someone's life? Perhaps you volunteer to read with children, do errands for seniors, or support a conservation or environmental group. Note at least one way you can be considerate of other people or things during the next few days. Then, jot down a message to yourself to help you remember to go out and do it.

Share my Blessings and Serve a Greater Good

I offer my skills, talents, and time freely and joy flows through me.

♥ ♥

SUNDAY

Date_____   Mood Check_____

Do you believe in the sacredness of all living creatures? If so, does this encourage you to share your blessings with others? Can you recall one special time when you were extremely generous? How did that make you feel? Write about it now.

Share my Blessings and Serve a Greater Good

I offer my skills, talents, and time freely and joy flows through me.

♥♥♥♥♥♥♥♥♥♥♥♥♥♥♥♥♥♥♥♥♥♥♥♥

Reflections for the Week

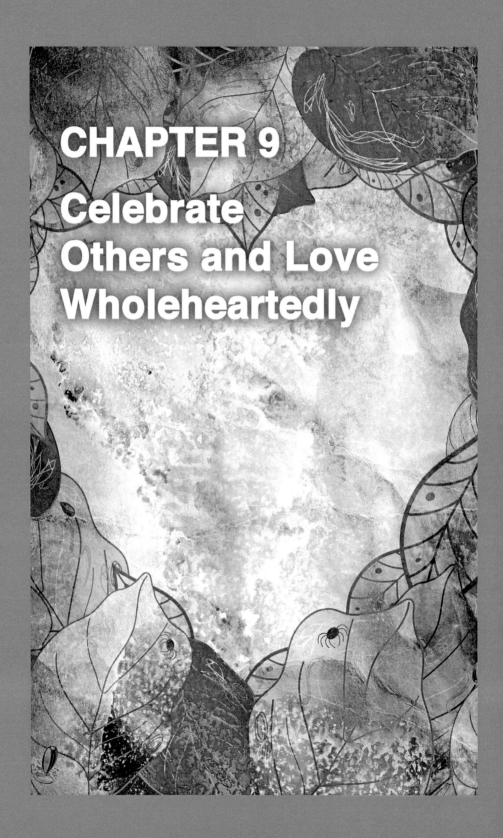

CHAPTER 9
Celebrate Others and Love Wholeheartedly

Celebrate Others and Love Wholeheartedly

I appreciate goodness in others and love unconditionally.

♥ ♥

MONDAY

Date_____   Mood Check_____

Please fill in the date and mood check-in spaces. Then, think of a color that signifies love and caring to you. Envision this color as you acknowledge the decency in other people and yourself. Do you usually give loved ones, friends, and strangers the benefit of the doubt when you see things differently than they do? Write about this topic now.

Celebrate Others and Love Wholeheartedly

I appreciate goodness in others and love unconditionally.

♥ ♥

TUESDAY

Date_____   Mood Check_____

Before you give unsolicited advice or take over a task for someone else, question your motives. Clarify your ideas by asking yourself whether telling someone what to do or stepping in to "rescue" them is serving you and the other person well. If help is not requested, don't give it. What kind words can you offer to show you have faith that the other person will find her/his own way? Explain.

Celebrate Others and Love Wholeheartedly

I appreciate goodness in others and love unconditionally.

♥ ♥

WEDNESDAY

Date_____   Mood Check_____

If you have young children, do you listen to their opinions as well as guide them along? If your children are grown or this does not apply, how do you assure your inner child (that young girl inside you) that her opinion is respected? Write about either subject now.

Celebrate Others and Love Wholeheartedly

I appreciate goodness in others and love unconditionally.

♥ ♥

THURSDAY

Date_____   Mood Check_____

When you engage in a conversation with another person, do you give that person your full attention? Before you answer, think if you interrupt the flow of communication by taking calls, looking at text or phone messages, or thinking of personal concerns. Then, write about your level of engagement here.

Celebrate Others and Love Wholeheartedly

I appreciate goodness in others and love unconditionally.

♥ ♥

FRIDAY

Date_____   Mood Check_____

Are you sincere and generous with compliments? Do you appreciate kindness, cheerfulness, and skillfulness in others? How can you express this? Please describe it now.

Celebrate Others and Love Wholeheartedly

I appreciate goodness in others and love unconditionally.

♥ ♥

SATURDAY

Date_____   Mood Check_____

How do you treat the people you work with? Are you considerate, respectful, and kind or do you frequently feel angry, put-upon, or threatened by those at your workplace? How do you treat people when you are driving, on line in the bank or supermarket, or anywhere you interact with others? Write about one of these topics now.

Celebrate Others and Love Wholeheartedly

I appreciate goodness in others and love unconditionally.

♥ ♥

SUNDAY

Date_____ Mood Check_____

When you respect all living things, you contribute to world harmony and peace. List the tangible ways you demonstrate your concern for people, animals, vegetation, and the environment of our planet. If you think you need work in any of these areas, what would motivate you to change? Write about this topic now.

Celebrate Others and Love Wholeheartedly

I appreciate goodness in others
and love unconditionally.

♥♥♥♥♥♥♥♥♥♥♥♥♥♥♥♥♥♥♥♥♥♥♥♥

Reflections for the Week

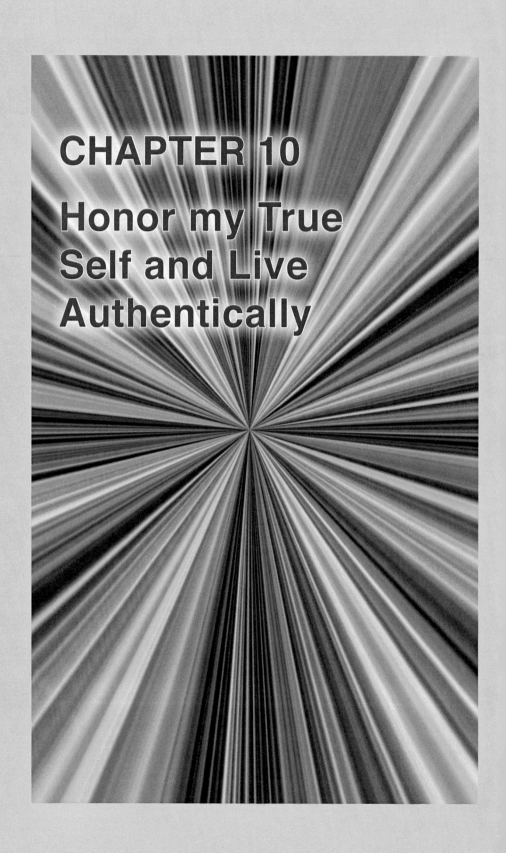

CHAPTER 10

Honor my True Self and Live Authentically

Honor my True Self and Live Authentically

I value myself and my actions express who I truly am.

♥ ♥

MONDAY

Date_____   Mood Check_____

What new facets of your personality have you discovered since you began this interactive guide? Recording your mood and re-checking it after journaling will help you recognize how often feelings change. Think of the colors yellow and green and image them dancing together. How have you grown, since you began *Colors of Joy*? Write about that now.

Honor my True Self and Live Authentically

I value myself and my actions express who I truly am.

♥ ♥

TUESDAY

Date_____   Mood Check_____

Before you decide to act, do you think about your motives? If you act impulsively and later regret it, pause long enough to imagine soft blue in your mind's eye. Know that this hue encourages calm, peace, and knowledge. Whenever you feel unsure, find comfort and stability by envisioning soft blue. Now, write about your decision-making skills and evaluate whether your behavior in this area serves you well.

Honor my True Self and Live Authentically

I value myself and my actions express who I truly am.

♥ ♥

WEDNESDAY

Date_____   Mood Check_____

Reflect about your personal conduct, values, and ethics. Do your actions and beliefs make you feel proud of yourself? Does your opinion of yourself count more to you than what others may think? Write about this now.

Honor my True Self and Live Authentically

I value myself and my actions express who I truly am.

♥ ♥

THURSDAY

Date_____   Mood Check_____

Are you willing to speak out for what you believe in? Do you stand up for your values and opinions, even though others may not agree? Explain.

Honor my True Self and Live Authentically
I value myself and my actions express who I truly am.

♥ ♥

FRIDAY

Date_____ Mood Check_____

For today, do something for yourself that you've been putting off, but are longing to do. Later on today or tomorrow, come back to this section. Describe what you felt or thought about while satisfying your yearning. Did this activity illustrate one way to live authentically? Please answer yes or no and explain why.

Honor my True Self and Live Authentically

I value myself and my actions express who I truly am.

♥ ♥

SATURDAY

Date_____   Mood Check_____

How do you show others that you respect and care about yourself? Do you feel others respect you and treat you well? Write about both questions; they are interrelated.

Honor my True Self and Live Authentically

I value myself and my actions express who I truly am.

♥ ♥

SUNDAY

Date_____   Mood Check_____

Are you honest with yourself, your family, friends, and business associates? Do you aspire to leave a lasting impressing on one person (to feel good about yourself) or many in your community, state, country, and world? Write about either topic now.

Honor my True Self and Live Authentically

I value myself and my actions express who I truly am.

♥♥♥♥♥♥♥♥♥♥♥♥♥♥♥♥♥♥♥♥♥♥♥♥♥

Reflections for the Week

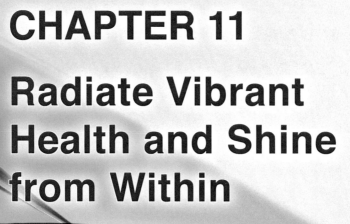

CHAPTER 11

Radiate Vibrant Health and Shine from Within

Radiate Vibrant Health and Shine from Within

I am a wondrous being who nurtures my mind, body, and spirit.

♥♥♥♥♥♥♥♥♥♥♥♥♥♥♥♥♥♥♥♥♥♥♥♥♥♥♥♥♥

MONDAY

Date_____   Mood Check_____

Take a moment to fill in the date and mood check areas. Do you satisfy your physical, mental, emotional, and spiritual needs on a consistent basis? If you slack off on self-care or think you're too busy to exercise, sleep, or daydream, you limit personal health possibilities. This week, schedule at least one nurturing activity each day. Affirm: *I enhance my personal well-being daily.* Remember to reserve time for it by recording it on your calendar. Follow through with the plan. In the space provided below, describe how grooming activities like hair care, massage, or a pedicure helps you relax and shine.

Radiate Vibrant Health and Shine from Within

I am a wondrous being who nurtures my mind, body, and spirit.

♥ ♥

TUESDAY

Date_____   Mood Check_____

When you feel strong emotions such as sadness, anger, loneliness, and fear, do you work through them in a healthful way? Envision the semi-precious stone, turquoise. It has been used for many centuries as an amulet for promoting health and strengthening one's body and self-confidence. How does knowing this and envisioning the color turquoise help you face your feelings? Explain.

Radiate Vibrant Health and Shine from Within

I am a wondrous being who nurtures my mind, body, and spirit.

♥♥♥♥♥♥♥♥♥♥♥♥♥♥♥♥♥♥♥♥♥♥♥♥♥♥

WEDNESDAY

Date_____   Mood Check_____

What feelings come up when you think about yourself as you are right now? Do you appreciate your assets? What places inside you need attention and what issues trouble you? What are you passionate about? Write about your fondest desires now.

Radiate Vibrant Health and Shine from Within

I am a wondrous being who nurtures my mind, body, and spirit.

♥ ♥

THURSDAY

Date_____   Mood Check_____

Do you know people whom you can talk with openly and honestly? List them below. If you're faced with a situation that bothers you, call or meet with someone on your list. If you lack emotional support, please consider looking into a twelve-step program or other form of support group. Another alternative is to speak with a clergy member or therapist. When a woman keeps things bottled up inside, it affects her health negatively. List all the avenues of help you know below. Then, earmark this page. Use it, if you forget you have options.

Radiate Vibrant Health and Shine from Within

I am a wondrous being who nurtures my mind, body, and spirit.

♥♥♥♥♥♥♥♥♥♥♥♥♥♥♥♥♥♥♥♥♥♥♥♥♥♥

FRIDAY

Date_____   Mood Check_____

Fill in the date and record your mood please. A walk in the woods, mountains, at the seashore, or in an open field can restore and renew your spirit. How? What makes you feel comforted? Incorporate at least one stress-reducing practice like trekking in nature, swimming, yoga, or biking into your schedule this week. What activities invigorate you? List them below. Evaluate your mood, after you finish journaling today.

Radiate Vibrant Health and Shine from Within

I am a wondrous being who nurtures my mind, body, and spirit.

♥♥♥♥♥♥♥♥♥♥♥♥♥♥♥♥♥♥♥♥♥♥♥♥♥

SATURDAY

Date_____   Mood Check_____

Today, accept you have choices. Do you want to hold on to emotional pain or release your grip? What worry, hurt, sadness, anger, or resentment do you want to release today and what small things can you do to make it happen? Write about it now as you envision white light flowing through you.

Radiate Vibrant Health and Shine from Within

I am a wondrous being who nurtures my mind, body, and spirit.

♥♥♥♥♥♥♥♥♥♥♥♥♥♥♥♥♥♥♥♥♥♥♥♥♥♥♥

SUNDAY

Date_____   Mood Check_____

Today, think of the color green and envision yourself in a plush green field of clover. Perhaps you'd enjoy eating a mouthwatering green salad for lunch. If you feel stressed, skip around in your bare feet for a few moments. If you prefer, take a two minute break, fifteen times today. Close your eyes and envision the sun as it rises in the sky. Then, visualize yourself as you tend to your health and happiness in the coming weeks. Write about the connection between self-care, renewed energy, and joy.

Radiate Vibrant Health and Shine from Within

I am a wondrous being who nurtures my mind, body, and spirit.

♥♥♥♥♥♥♥♥♥♥♥♥♥♥♥♥♥♥♥♥♥♥♥♥♥

Reflections for the Week

CHAPTER 12

Connect to the Source and Renew my Spirit

Connect to the Source and Renew my Spirit
My life force sustains me and love blooms in my life.

♥♥♥♥♥♥♥♥♥♥♥♥♥♥♥♥♥♥♥♥♥♥♥♥♥♥♥

MONDAY

Date_____   Mood Check_____

Please fill in the blanks for the date and mood check. Then, envision the color called indigo. It's the color of the deep night sky. This hue helps promote understanding, insights, and spiritual energy. Do you trust in some force, whether it is God, nature, humanity, or a Higher Power that sustains you? Write about your beliefs.

Connect to the Source and Renew my Spirit
My life force sustains me and love blooms in my life.

♥♥♥♥♥♥♥♥♥♥♥♥♥♥♥♥♥♥♥♥♥♥♥♥♥♥

TUESDAY

Date_____   Mood Check_____

Life sometimes feels lonely, difficult, confusing, or troubling. Remind yourself that it is a basic need to have human contact. Every woman is entitled to and deserves support from others. Today, even if you think you don't need it, reach out to someone and ask for a hug or smile. Write about how this assignment makes you feel.

Connect to the Source and Renew my Spirit
My life force sustains me and love blooms in my life.

♥♥♥♥♥♥♥♥♥♥♥♥♥♥♥♥♥♥♥♥♥♥♥♥♥♥

WEDNESDAY

Date_____   Mood Check_____

When you're at odds with yourself, try this. Look at yourself with loving kindness, and "act as if" you are your own best friend. Practice affirming you are worthy, especially if you are in the habit of undervaluing yourself. Write about trust in yourself now.

Connect to the Source and Renew my Spirit
My life force sustains me and love blooms in my life.

♥♥♥♥♥♥♥♥♥♥♥♥♥♥♥♥♥♥♥♥♥♥♥♥♥

THURSDAY

Date_____   Mood Check_____

Do you realize that "lack" is an illusion? Say this affirmation aloud: *I know all my needs are met and my spirit prospers right now.* In what ways can this affirmation lessen your worry or change negative thoughts? Write about it now.

Connect to the Source and Renew my Spirit

My life force sustains me and love blooms in my life.

♥♥♥♥♥♥♥♥♥♥♥♥♥♥♥♥♥♥♥♥♥♥♥♥♥♥♥

FRIDAY

Date_____   Mood Check_____

Don't forget to record your mood before and after this activity. Do you believe in God, Goddess, or the grandeur of nature? Perhaps you identify with a power within that touches you each time you hear a child's laughter or smell a spring rain. Maybe you feel spirit when you shed healing tears. Do you believe in the energy of community, family, goodness, love, or yourself? Write about faith now.

Connect to the Source and Renew my Spirit
My life force sustains me and love blooms in my life.
♥♥♥♥♥♥♥♥♥♥♥♥♥♥♥♥♥♥♥♥♥♥♥♥♥♥
SATURDAY

Date_____   Mood Check_____

Today, envision the color indigo. This midnight blue shade is associated with the sixth chakra, located in the space between your eyebrows. Indigo helps you tap into your intuition and spiritual knowledge. Have you developed a spiritual practice or have none? Answer this question now. Then, describe activities like meditation, prayer, yoga, music, art, dance, or other healing arts that help you experience a sense of unity, serenity, and bliss. If you need more space for journaling, use the reflections area at the end of this chapter.

Connect to the Source and Renew my Spirit

My life force sustains me and love blooms in my life.

♥♥♥♥♥♥♥♥♥♥♥♥♥♥♥♥♥♥♥♥♥♥♥♥♥♥

SUNDAY

Date_____   Mood Check_____

Jot down today's date and your mood in the spaces provided. Read the next statement aloud, please. *Unlimited Abundance and Oneness flows through me and I am centered, joyful, and free.* What life affirming activities can you engage in today? List them now. Then do them.

Connect to the Source and Renew my Spirit

My life force sustains me and love blooms in my life.

♥♥♥♥♥♥♥♥♥♥♥♥♥♥♥♥♥♥♥♥♥♥♥♥♥

Reflections for the Week

♥ ♥ ♥ Musings, Doodles, and Insights ♥ ♥ ♥

Please use the space on this page as well as the next one for creative expression. Have fun drawing or writing with colored pencils, markers, paint, and art supplies.

♥♥♥ Musings, Doodles, and Insights ♥♥♥

Additional Reading

10 Steps to Take Charge of Your Emotional Life: Overcoming Anxiety, Distress, and Depression through Whole-Person Healing (In One), Eve Wood, M.D. Hay House Inc., Carlsbad, CA 2008

A Practical Guide to Vibrational Medicine: Energy Healing and Spiritual Transformation, Richard Gerber, M.D. Harper Collins, New York, NY 2000

Authentic Happiness: Using the New Positive Psychology to Realize Your Potential for Lasting Fulfillment, Martin Seligman, Ph.D., Atria Books (Simon & Schuster) New York, NY 2004.

Colours of the Soul: Transform Your Life Through Color Therapy, June McLeod, John Hunt Publishing, Oxford, UK 2007

Daring Greatly: How the Courage to Be Vulnerable Transforms the Way We Live, Love, Parent, and Lead, Brené Brown, Ph.D., Gotham Books, New York, NY 2012

Healing Color for Health and Well Being: How to harness the power of color to transform your mind, body and spirit, Lilian Verner Bonds, Anness Publishing Ltd., London, UK 2008

How to Heal with Color (How To Series), Ted Andrews. Llewellyn Publications, Woodbury, MN 2005

How You Feel Is Up To You: the Power of Emotional Choice, Gary D. McKay and Don Dinkmeyer. Impact Publishers, Inc. Atascadero, CA, 2002.

Journey to the Self: Twenty-Two Paths to Personal Growth, Kathleen Adams. Warner Books, New York, NY 1990

Learned Optimism: How to Change Your Mind and Your Life, Martin Seligman, Ph.D., Vintage, New York, NY 2006

Seven Spiritual Laws of Success, Deepak Chopra, Hay House, Inc., Carlsbad, CA 2008

The Creative Visualization Workbook, Shakti Gawain, New World Library, Novato, CA 1995

The Dance of Anger: a Woman's Guide to Changing the Pattern of Intimate Relationships, Harriet Lerner, Ph.D., Harper Collins, New York, NY 2005

The Extraordinary Healing Power of Ordinary Things Fourteen Natural Steps to Health & Happiness, Larry Dossey M.D., Harmony Books (Imprint Crown Publishing Group, a division of Random House, Inc.), New York, NY 2006

The Happiness Project: Or, Why I Spent a Year Trying to Sing in the Morning, Clean My Closets, Fight Right, Read Aristotle, and Generally Have More Fun, Gretchen Rubin, Harper Paperbacks (Imprint of Harper Collins Publishers), New York, NY 2011

The Healing Power of Color: Using Color to Improve Your Mental, Physical, and Spiritual Well-Being by Betty Wood, Inner Traditions International Ltd., VT 1998

The Practical Book of Color Therapy, Susan and Simon Lilly, Southwater (Imprint of Annes Publishing Ltd.), London, UK 2001 & 2009

The Relaxation & Stress Reduction Workbook, Martha Davis, Ph.D., Elizabeth Robbins Eshelman, M.S.W., Matthew McKay, Ph.D., New Harbinger Publications, Inc. Oakland, CA 2008

The Way of the Journal: A Journal Therapy Workbook for Healing, Kathleen Adams, M.A., L.P.C., Sidran Press, Brooklandville, MD. 1998

The Wisdom of Menopause: Creating Physical and Emotional Health and Healing During the Change, Christiane Northrup M.D., Bantam, New York, NY 2012

Women's Bodies, Women's Wisdom Creating Physical and Emotional Health and Healing, Christiane Northrup M.D., Bantam, New York, NY 2010

You Can Heal Your Life, Louise L. Hay, Hay House, Inc., Carlsbad, CA 2012

About the Author and Therapist

Nancy Andres, B.S. is a Health & Lifestyle Writer and Blogger. For the past 20 years, Nancy has researched, observed, and studied numerous colors and how they influence peoples' emotions and thinking. In addition, she has investigated the impact specific colors have on home furnishings, business related objects, clothing, food, and lifestyle choices. Her articles, reports, and essays have been published in presses including **The New York Times, Newsday, American Profile Magazine,** and **Lovin' Life After 50.** "Facing the Fire," an essay selected from hundreds of entries, appeared in the Adams Media anthology, *Changing Course: Women's Inspiring Stories of Menopause, Midlife, and Moving Forward.* Nancy celebrates life with her husband Steven, in Tucson, Arizona.

Please visit her at www.nancyandreswriter.com,

http://obloggernewbie.blogspot.com, and

http://www.nancyandreswriter.com/colors-of-joy-blog

Kay Lesh, Ph.D. Kay is an educator and psychotherapist, licensed by the State of Arizona as a Marriage and Family Therapist. Two of the many books she has coauthored are *Our Money Ourselves for Couples: A New Way of Relating to Money and Each Other,* and *Building Self Esteem.*